BY STACY B. DAVIDS

Reading Consultant:
Barbara J. Fox
Reading Specialist
North Carolina State University

CAPSTONE PRESS
a capstone imprint

Blazers is published by Capstone Press,
151 Good Counsel Drive, P.O. Box 669, Mankato, Minnesota 56002.
www.capstonepub.com

Books published by Capstone Press are manufactured with paper
containing at least 10 percent post-consumer waste.

Library of Congress Cataloging-in-Publication Data
Davids, Stacy B.
  Strange but true weather / by Stacy B. Davids.
    p. cm. — (Blazers. Strange but true)
  Summary: "Describes unusual weather events"—Provided by publisher.
  Includes bibliographical references and index.
  ISBN 978-1-4296-4553-9 (library binding)
  1. Weather—Miscellanea—Juvenile literature. I. Title. II. Series.
  QC981.3.D358 2011
  551.6—dc22   2010000998

Editorial Credits
Editor: Kathryn Clay
Designer: Kyle Grenz
Media Researcher: Svetlana Zhurkin
Production Specialist: Laura Manthe

Photo Credits
Alamy/Phototake/Gene Moore, 22–23; Robbie Shone, 12–13; Tom Uhlman, cover
AP Images/Chillicothe Gazette/Martin S. Lerman, 14–15
Corbis, 6–7
Dreamstime/Chris White, 26–27; Victor Zastolskiy, 8–9
Getty Images/David McNew, 20–21; National Geographic/Norbert Rosing, 24–25
Landov/UPI/Carlos Gutierrez, 28–29
Shutterstock/Andrejs Pidjass, cover (texture); Craig Hanson, 4–5; lfstewart, 10–11; Norma G.
    Chambers, 18–19
Visuals Unlimited/Doug Sokell, 16–17

TABLE OF CONTENTS

WACKY WEATHER

Clouds that look like **UFOs**. Fish falling from the sky. **Tornadoes** made of fire. These weather events may sound strange. But they are all true.

UFO—an object in the sky thought to be a spaceship from another planet

tornado—a violent, spinning column of air that looks like a funnel

5

VOLCANIC LIGHTNING

Lightning doesn't just come from the sky. It is also made by volcanoes. When a volcano **erupts**, bits of hot dust crash into each other. The crashing dust creates volcanic lightning.

erupt—to burst out suddenly with great force

STRANGE but TRUE

Waterspouts like this one can shoot fish, frogs, and lizards into the air.

WATERSPOUTS

Grab a bucket instead of an umbrella. It's raining fish! **Waterspouts** can suck up fish and other small animals. The animals are tossed into the air. They fall like rain.

waterspout—a mass of spinning water and wind that stretches from a cloud to a body of water

UFO CLOUDS

Think you've seen a UFO? It's possible you really saw a **lenticular** cloud. People often mistake these clouds for UFOs. The clouds are shaped like discs. They usually form near mountains.

lenticular—smooth and disc-shaped

BLOOD RAIN

Windstorms carry red dust from the Sahara desert across Europe and India. When the dust mixes with rain clouds, dark red rain falls. The rain looks like blood pouring from the sky.

People have also reported seeing black, green, and yellow rain.

SNOW ROLLERS

Snow rollers are rare. Snow, wind, and ice combine to make huge snowballs. Wind pushes a clump of snow along the icy ground. The roller grows larger as it grabs more snow.

Sometimes snow rollers form holes in the middle. These rollers are called snow donuts.

DRY RAIN

Dry rain is also called virga.

Did you know it's possible to stand under rain clouds and not get wet? Dry air below the clouds can cause rain to **evaporate** before hitting the ground.

evaporate—to change from a liquid into a gas

NORTHERN LIGHTS

Colorful lights stream across the northern sky. The lights are made by tiny **particles**. When the particles hit Earth's **atmosphere**, they glow green, white, and red.

particle—a tiny piece of something

atmosphere—the mixture of gases that surrounds Earth

STRANGE *but* TRUE

Northern lights can be seen only from the northern parts of Earth.

FIRE WHIRLS

Fire whirls spin like tops. They can stay in one spot or zoom along the ground. These burning towers are made by powerful wildfires and strong winds.

Fire whirls are as dangerous
as small tornadoes.

ICE BOMBS

Imagine hail the size of grapefruits. Water freezes on hail in clouds. Sometimes hailstones stay in clouds for a long time. The longer hail stays in a cloud, the larger it grows.

Giant hail damages crops and cars. Hailstones have killed people and animals.

SUN DOGS

sun dog

Sun dogs are like rainbows. They appear as bright bands of light on the sides of the sun. Sun dogs are made when sunlight hits ice crystals.

SUPERCELLS

A huge, dark supercell looms overhead. This is the most dangerous kind of thunderstorm. Air rolls, rises, and spins. Supercells cause heavy rain, hail, lightning, and tornadoes.

STRANGE but TRUE

Supercell storms can last for hours and travel hundreds of miles.

WEATHERING the STORM

Weather events happen all over the world. They may be dangerous or harmless, scary or shocking. But good or bad, strange weather affects people each day.

GLOSSARY

atmosphere (AT-muh-sfeer)—the mixture of gases that surrounds Earth

erupt (i-RUHPT)—to burst out suddenly with great force

evaporate (i-VA-puh-rayt)—to change from a liquid into a gas

hail (HAYL)—balls of ice that form in clouds and fall to the ground

lenticular (len-TIK-yuh-lur)—smooth and disc-shaped

particle (PAR-tuh-kuhl)—a tiny piece of something

tornado (tor-NAY-doh)—a violent, spinning column of air that looks like a funnel

UFO (YOO EF OH)—an object in the sky thought to be a spaceship from another planet; UFO is short for Unidentified Flying Object

waterspout (WAW-tur-spowt)—a mass of spinning water and wind that stretches from a cloud to a body of water

READ MORE

Birch, Robin. *Extreme Weather*. Weather and Climate.
New York: Marshall Cavendish Benchmark, 2009.

Levete, Sarah. *Catastrophic Weather*. Protecting Our Planet.
New York: Crabtree, 2010.

Miller, Connie Colwell. *The Deadliest Weather on Earth*. The
World's Deadliest. Mankato, Minn.: Capstone Press, 2010.

INTERNET SITES

FactHound offers a safe, fun way to find Internet sites
related to this book. All of the sites on FactHound have
been researched by our staff.

Here's all you do:

Visit *www.facthound.com*

FactHound will fetch the best sites for you!

INDEX